ILLUMINATED SCRIPTURE JOURNAL

ENGLISH STANDARD VERSION

ZEPHANIAH, HAGGAI, ZECHARIAH, AND MALACHI

WHEATON, ILLINOIS — ESV.ORG

ESV® Illuminated Scripture Journal: Zephaniah, Haggai, Zechariah, and Malachi
The Holy Bible, English Standard Version® (ESV®)
Copyright © 2001 by Crossway,
a publishing ministry of Good News Publishers.
All rights reserved.
ESV® Text Edition: 2016

Permissions notice: The ESV text may be quoted (in written, visual, or electronic form) up to and inclusive of five hundred (500) consecutive verses without express written permission of the publisher, provided that the verses quoted do not amount to more than one-half of any one book of the Bible or its equivalent measured in bytes and provided that the verses quoted do not account for twenty-five percent (25%) or more of the total text of the work in which they are quoted.

The ESV text may be quoted for audio use (audio cassettes, CDs, audio television) up to five hundred (500) verses without express written permission of the publisher, provided that the verses quoted do not amount to more than one-half of any one book of the Bible or its equivalent measured in bytes and provided that the verses quoted do not account for twenty-five percent (25%) or more of the total text of the work in which they are quoted.

Notice of copyright must appear as follows on the title page or copyright page of printed works quoting from the ESV, or in a corresponding location when the ESV is quoted in other media:

"Scripture quotations are from The ESV® Bible (The Holy Bible, English Standard Version®), copyright © 2001 by Crossway, a publishing ministry of Good News Publishers. Used by permission. All rights reserved."

When more than one translation is quoted in printed works or other media, the foregoing notice of copyright should begin as follows:

"Unless otherwise indicated, all Scripture quotations are from . . . [etc.]"; or,
"Scripture quotations marked (ESV) are from . . . [etc.]."

The "ESV" and "English Standard Version" are registered trademarks of Crossway. Use of either trademark requires the permission of Crossway.

When quotations from the ESV text are used in non-saleable print and digital media, such as church bulletins, orders of service, posters, transparencies, or similar media, a complete copyright notice is not required, but the initials (ESV) must appear at the end of the quotation.

Publication of any commentary or other Bible reference work produced for commercial sale that uses the English Standard Version (ESV) must include written permission for use of the ESV text.

Permission requests that exceed the above guidelines must be directed to Crossway, Attn: Bible Rights, 1300 Crescent Street, Wheaton, IL 60187, USA.

Permission requests for use of the anglicized ESV Bible text that exceed the above guidelines must be directed to: HarperCollins Religious, The News Building, 1 London Bridge Street, London SE1 9GF, UK.

Supplemental material: The ESV Preface and headings in the Bible text, copyright © 2001 by Crossway. Illustrations copyright © 2017 by Dana Tanamachi. Used and adapted with permission. All rights reserved.

The Holy Bible, English Standard Version (ESV) is adapted from the Revised Standard Version of the Bible, copyright Division of Christian Education of the National Council of the Churches of Christ in the U.S.A. All rights reserved.

Printed in China
Published by Crossway
Wheaton, Illinois 60187, U.S.A.
crossway.org

Crossway is a not-for-profit publishing ministry that exists solely for the purpose of publishing the Good News of the Gospel and the Truth of God's Word, the Bible. A portion of the purchase price of every ESV Bible is donated to help support Bible distribution ministry around the world.

The ESV Bible is free online and on mobile devices everywhere worldwide, including a selection of free Bible resources, at esv.org.

RRDS	28	27	26	25	24
12	11	10	9	8	

PREFACE

The Bible

The words of the Bible are the very words of God our Creator speaking to us. They are completely truthful;[1] they are pure;[2] they are powerful;[3] and they are wise and righteous.[4] We should read these words with reverence and awe,[5] and with joy and delight.[6] Through these words God gives us eternal life,[7] and daily nourishes our spiritual lives.[8]

The ESV Translation

The English Standard Version® (ESV®) stands in the classic stream of English Bible translations that goes back nearly five centuries. In this stream, accurate faithfulness to the original text is combined with simplicity, beauty, and dignity of expression. Our goal has been to carry forward this legacy for this generation and generations to come.

The ESV is an "essentially literal" translation that seeks as far as possible to reproduce the meaning and structure of the original text and the personal style of each Bible writer. We have sought to be "as literal as possible" while maintaining clear expression and literary excellence. Therefore the ESV is well suited for both personal reading and church ministry, for devotional reflection and serious study, and for Scripture memorization.

---

[1] Ps. 119:160; Prov. 30:5; Titus 1:2; Heb. 6:18 [2] Ps. 12:6 [3] Jer. 23:29; Heb. 4:12; 1 Pet. 1:23
[4] Ps. 19:7–11 [5] Deut. 28:58; Ps. 119:74; Isa. 66:2 [6] Ps. 19:7–11; 119:14, 97, 103; Jer. 15:16
[7] John 6:68; 1 Pet. 1:23 [8] Deut. 32:46; Matt. 4:4

The ESV Publishing Team

The ESV publishing team has included more than a hundred people. The fourteen-member Translation Oversight Committee benefited from the work of fifty biblical experts serving as Translation Review Scholars and from the comments of the more than fifty members of the Advisory Council. This international team from many denominations shares a common commitment to the truth of God's Word and to historic Christian orthodoxy.

To God's Honor and Praise

We know that no Bible translation is perfect; but we also know that God uses imperfect and inadequate things to his honor and praise. So to God the Father, Son, and Holy Spirit—and to his people—we offer what we have done, with our prayers that it may prove useful, with gratitude for much help given, and with ongoing wonder that our God should ever have entrusted to us so momentous a task.

To God alone be the glory!
The Translation Oversight Committee

ZEPHANIAH

1 The word of the LORD that came to Zephaniah the son of Cushi, son of Gedaliah, son of Amariah, son of Hezekiah, in the days of Josiah the son of Amon, king of Judah.

The Coming Judgment on Judah

2   "I will utterly sweep away everything
      from the face of the earth," declares the LORD.
3   "I will sweep away man and beast;
      I will sweep away the birds of the heavens
      and the fish of the sea,
   and the rubble with the wicked.
      I will cut off mankind
      from the face of the earth," declares the LORD.
4   "I will stretch out my hand against Judah
      and against all the inhabitants of Jerusalem;
   and I will cut off from this place the remnant of Baal
      and the name of the idolatrous priests along
          with the priests,
5   those who bow down on the roofs
      to the host of the heavens,
   those who bow down and swear to the LORD
      and yet swear by Milcom,
6   those who have turned back from following the LORD,
      who do not seek the LORD or inquire of him."

The Day of the Lord Is Near

7 Be silent before the Lord God!
 For the day of the Lord is near;
 the Lord has prepared a sacrifice
 and consecrated his guests.
8 And on the day of the Lord's sacrifice—
 "I will punish the officials and the king's sons
 and all who array themselves in foreign attire.
9 On that day I will punish
 everyone who leaps over the threshold,
 and those who fill their master's house
 with violence and fraud.

10 "On that day," declares the Lord,
 "a cry will be heard from the Fish Gate,
 a wail from the Second Quarter,
 a loud crash from the hills.
11 Wail, O inhabitants of the Mortar!
 For all the traders are no more;
 all who weigh out silver are cut off.
12 At that time I will search Jerusalem with lamps,
 and I will punish the men
 who are complacent,
 those who say in their hearts,
 'The Lord will not do good,
 nor will he do ill.'
13 Their goods shall be plundered,
 and their houses laid waste.
 Though they build houses,
 they shall not inhabit them;

> though they plant vineyards,
>> they shall not drink wine from them."

14 The great day of the Lord is near,
>> near and hastening fast;
> the sound of the day of the Lord is bitter;
>> the mighty man cries aloud there.
15 A day of wrath is that day,
>> a day of distress and anguish,
> a day of ruin and devastation,
>> a day of darkness and gloom,
> a day of clouds and thick darkness,
16 >> a day of trumpet blast and battle cry
> against the fortified cities
>> and against the lofty battlements.

17 I will bring distress on mankind,
>> so that they shall walk like the blind,
>> because they have sinned against the Lord;
> their blood shall be poured out like dust,
>> and their flesh like dung.
18 Neither their silver nor their gold
>> shall be able to deliver them
>> on the day of the wrath of the Lord.
> In the fire of his jealousy,
>> all the earth shall be consumed;
> for a full and sudden end
>> he will make of all the inhabitants of the earth.

Judgment on Judah's Enemies

2 Gather together, yes, gather,
O shameless nation,
² before the decree takes effect
—before the day passes away like chaff—
before there comes upon you
the burning anger of the Lord,
before there comes upon you
the day of the anger of the Lord.
³ Seek the Lord, all you humble of the land,
who do his just commands;
seek righteousness; seek humility;
perhaps you may be hidden
on the day of the anger of the Lord.
⁴ For Gaza shall be deserted,
and Ashkelon shall become a desolation;
Ashdod's people shall be driven out at noon,
and Ekron shall be uprooted.

⁵ Woe to you inhabitants of the seacoast,
you nation of the Cherethites!
The word of the Lord is against you,
O Canaan, land of the Philistines;
and I will destroy you until no inhabitant is left.
⁶ And you, O seacoast, shall be pastures,
with meadows for shepherds
and folds for flocks.
⁷ The seacoast shall become the possession
of the remnant of the house of Judah,
on which they shall graze,

  and in the houses of Ashkelon
    they shall lie down at evening.
 For the LORD their God will be mindful of them
   and restore their fortunes.

8 "I have heard the taunts of Moab
   and the revilings of the Ammonites,
 how they have taunted my people
   and made boasts against their territory.
9 Therefore, as I live," declares the LORD of hosts,
   the God of Israel,
"Moab shall become like Sodom,
   and the Ammonites like Gomorrah,
a land possessed by nettles and salt pits,
   and a waste forever.
The remnant of my people shall plunder them,
   and the survivors of my nation shall possess
    them."
10 This shall be their lot in return for their pride,
   because they taunted and boasted
  against the people of the LORD of hosts.
11 The LORD will be awesome against them;
   for he will famish all the gods of the
    earth,
 and to him shall bow down,
   each in its place,
   all the lands of the nations.

12 You also, O Cushites,
   shall be slain by my sword.

13 And he will stretch out his hand against the north
      and destroy Assyria,
  and he will make Nineveh a desolation,
      a dry waste like the desert.
14 Herds shall lie down in her midst,
      all kinds of beasts;
  even the owl and the hedgehog
      shall lodge in her capitals;
  a voice shall hoot in the window;
      devastation will be on the threshold;
      for her cedar work will be laid bare.
15 This is the exultant city
      that lived securely,
  that said in her heart,
      "I am, and there is no one else."
  What a desolation she has become,
      a lair for wild beasts!
  Everyone who passes by her
      hisses and shakes his fist.

Judgment on Jerusalem and the Nations

3 Woe to her who is rebellious and defiled,
  the oppressing city!
2   She listens to no voice;
      she accepts no correction.
  She does not trust in the LORD;
      she does not draw near to her God.

3   Her officials within her
      are roaring lions;

>   her judges are evening wolves
> > that leave nothing till the morning.
> 4 Her prophets are fickle, treacherous men;
>   her priests profane what is holy;
> > they do violence to the law.
> 5 The Lord within her is righteous;
> > he does no injustice;
>   every morning he shows forth his justice;
>   each dawn he does not fail;
>   but the unjust knows no shame.
>
> 6 "I have cut off nations;
> > their battlements are in ruins;
>   I have laid waste their streets
> > so that no one walks in them;
>   their cities have been made desolate,
> > without a man, without an inhabitant.
> 7 I said, 'Surely you will fear me;
> > you will accept correction.
>   Then your dwelling would not be cut off
> > according to all that I have appointed against you.'
>   But all the more they were eager
> > to make all their deeds corrupt.
>
> 8 "Therefore wait for me," declares the Lord,
> > "for the day when I rise up to seize the prey.
>   For my decision is to gather nations,
> > to assemble kingdoms,
>   to pour out upon them my indignation,
> > all my burning anger;

for in the fire of my jealousy
      all the earth shall be consumed.

The Conversion of the Nations

9 "For at that time I will change the speech of the peoples
      to a pure speech,
   that all of them may call upon the name of the Lord
      and serve him with one accord.
10 From beyond the rivers of Cush
      my worshipers, the daughter of my dispersed
         ones,
   shall bring my offering.

11 "On that day you shall not be put to shame
      because of the deeds by which you have rebelled
         against me;
   for then I will remove from your midst
      your proudly exultant ones,
   and you shall no longer be haughty
      in my holy mountain.
12 But I will leave in your midst
      a people humble and lowly.
   They shall seek refuge in the name of the Lord,
13   those who are left in Israel;
   they shall do no injustice
      and speak no lies,
   nor shall there be found in their mouth
      a deceitful tongue.
   For they shall graze and lie down,
      and none shall make them afraid."

Israel's Joy and Restoration

14 Sing aloud, O daughter of Zion;
   shout, O Israel!
Rejoice and exult with all your heart,
   O daughter of Jerusalem!
15 The LORD has taken away the judgments
      against you;
   he has cleared away your enemies.
The King of Israel, the LORD, is in your
      midst;
   you shall never again fear evil.
16 On that day it shall be said to Jerusalem:
"Fear not, O Zion;
   let not your hands grow weak.
17 The LORD your God is in your midst,
   a mighty one who will save;
he will rejoice over you with gladness;
   he will quiet you by his love;
he will exult over you with loud singing.
18 I will gather those of you who mourn for the
      festival,
   so that you will no longer suffer reproach.
19 Behold, at that time I will deal
   with all your oppressors.
And I will save the lame
   and gather the outcast,
and I will change their shame into praise
   and renown in all the earth.
20 At that time I will bring you in,
   at the time when I gather you together;

>   for I will make you renowned and praised
>   among all the peoples of the earth,
>   when I restore your fortunes
>   before your eyes," says the Lord.

HAGGAI

The Command to Rebuild the Temple

1 In the second year of Darius the king, in the sixth month, on the first day of the month, the word of the LORD came by the hand of Haggai the prophet to Zerubbabel the son of Shealtiel, governor of Judah, and to Joshua the son of Jehozadak, the high priest: ² "Thus says the LORD of hosts: These people say the time has not yet come to rebuild the house of the LORD." ³ Then the word of the LORD came by the hand of Haggai the prophet, ⁴ "Is it a time for you yourselves to dwell in your paneled houses, while this house lies in ruins? ⁵ Now, therefore, thus says the LORD of hosts: Consider your ways. ⁶ You have sown much, and harvested little. You eat, but you never have enough; you drink, but you never have your fill. You clothe yourselves, but no one is warm. And he who earns wages does so to put them into a bag with holes.

⁷ "Thus says the LORD of hosts: Consider your ways. ⁸ Go up to the hills and bring wood and build the house, that I may take pleasure in it and that I may be glorified, says the LORD. ⁹ You looked for much, and behold, it came to little. And when you brought it home, I blew it away. Why? declares the LORD of hosts. Because of my house that lies in ruins, while each of you busies himself with his own house. ¹⁰ Therefore the heavens above you have withheld the dew, and the earth has withheld

its produce. ¹¹ And I have called for a drought on the land and the hills, on the grain, the new wine, the oil, on what the ground brings forth, on man and beast, and on all their labors."

The People Obey the LORD

¹² Then Zerubbabel the son of Shealtiel, and Joshua the son of Jehozadak, the high priest, with all the remnant of the people, obeyed the voice of the LORD their God, and the words of Haggai the prophet, as the LORD their God had sent him. And the people feared the LORD. ¹³ Then Haggai, the messenger of the LORD, spoke to the people with the LORD's message, "I am with you, declares the LORD." ¹⁴ And the LORD stirred up the spirit of Zerubbabel the son of Shealtiel, governor of Judah, and the spirit of Joshua the son of Jehozadak, the high priest, and the spirit of all the remnant of the people. And they came and worked on the house of the LORD of hosts, their God, ¹⁵ on the twenty-fourth day of the month, in the sixth month, in the second year of Darius the king.

The Coming Glory of the Temple

2 In the seventh month, on the twenty-first day of the month, the word of the LORD came by the hand of Haggai the prophet: ² "Speak now to Zerubbabel the son of Shealtiel, governor of Judah, and to Joshua the son of Jehozadak, the high priest, and to all the remnant of the people, and say, ³ 'Who is left among you who saw this house in its former glory? How do you see it now? Is it not as nothing in your eyes? ⁴ Yet now be strong, O Zerubbabel, declares the LORD. Be strong, O Joshua, son of Jehozadak, the high priest. Be strong, all you people of the land, declares the LORD. Work, for I am with you, declares

the Lord of hosts, ⁵ according to the covenant that I made with you when you came out of Egypt. My Spirit remains in your midst. Fear not. ⁶ For thus says the Lord of hosts: Yet once more, in a little while, I will shake the heavens and the earth and the sea and the dry land. ⁷ And I will shake all nations, so that the treasures of all nations shall come in, and I will fill this house with glory, says the Lord of hosts. ⁸ The silver is mine, and the gold is mine, declares the Lord of hosts. ⁹ The latter glory of this house shall be greater than the former, says the Lord of hosts. And in this place I will give peace, declares the Lord of hosts.'"

Blessings for a Defiled People

¹⁰ On the twenty-fourth day of the ninth month, in the second year of Darius, the word of the Lord came by Haggai the prophet, ¹¹ "Thus says the Lord of hosts: Ask the priests about the law: ¹² 'If someone carries holy meat in the fold of his garment and touches with his fold bread or stew or wine or oil or any kind of food, does it become holy?'" The priests answered and said, "No." ¹³ Then Haggai said, "If someone who is unclean by contact with a dead body touches any of these, does it become unclean?" The priests answered and said, "It does become unclean." ¹⁴ Then Haggai answered and said, "So is it with this people, and with this nation before me, declares the Lord, and so with every work of their hands. And what they offer there is unclean. ¹⁵ Now then, consider from this day onward. Before stone was placed upon stone in the temple of the Lord, ¹⁶ how did you fare? When one came to a heap of twenty measures, there were but ten. When one came to the wine vat to draw fifty measures, there were but twenty.

¹⁷ I struck you and all the products of your toil with blight and with mildew and with hail, yet you did not turn to me, declares the Lord. ¹⁸ Consider from this day onward, from the twenty-fourth day of the ninth month. Since the day that the foundation of the Lord's temple was laid, consider: ¹⁹ Is the seed yet in the barn? Indeed, the vine, the fig tree, the pomegranate, and the olive tree have yielded nothing. But from this day on I will bless you."

Zerubbabel Chosen as a Signet

²⁰ The word of the Lord came a second time to Haggai on the twenty-fourth day of the month, ²¹ "Speak to Zerubbabel, governor of Judah, saying, I am about to shake the heavens and the earth, ²² and to overthrow the throne of kingdoms. I am about to destroy the strength of the kingdoms of the nations, and overthrow the chariots and their riders. And the horses and their riders shall go down, every one by the sword of his brother. ²³ On that day, declares the Lord of hosts, I will take you, O Zerubbabel my servant, the son of Shealtiel, declares the Lord, and make you like a signet ring, for I have chosen you, declares the Lord of hosts."

ZECHARIAH

A Call to Return to the Lord

1 In the eighth month, in the second year of Darius, the word of the Lord came to the prophet Zechariah, the son of Berechiah, son of Iddo, saying, ²"The Lord was very angry with your fathers. ³Therefore say to them, Thus declares the Lord of hosts: Return to me, says the Lord of hosts, and I will return to you, says the Lord of hosts. ⁴Do not be like your fathers, to whom the former prophets cried out, 'Thus says the Lord of hosts, Return from your evil ways and from your evil deeds.' But they did not hear or pay attention to me, declares the Lord. ⁵Your fathers, where are they? And the prophets, do they live forever? ⁶But my words and my statutes, which I commanded my servants the prophets, did they not overtake your fathers? So they repented and said, 'As the Lord of hosts purposed to deal with us for our ways and deeds, so has he dealt with us.'"

A Vision of a Horseman

⁷On the twenty-fourth day of the eleventh month, which is the month of Shebat, in the second year of Darius, the word of the Lord came to the prophet Zechariah, the son of Berechiah, son of Iddo, saying, ⁸"I saw in the night, and behold, a man riding on a red horse! He was standing among the myrtle trees in the glen, and behind him were red, sorrel, and white

horses. ⁹ Then I said, 'What are these, my lord?' The angel who talked with me said to me, 'I will show you what they are.' ¹⁰ So the man who was standing among the myrtle trees answered, 'These are they whom the LORD has sent to patrol the earth.' ¹¹ And they answered the angel of the LORD who was standing among the myrtle trees, and said, 'We have patrolled the earth, and behold, all the earth remains at rest.' ¹² Then the angel of the LORD said, 'O LORD of hosts, how long will you have no mercy on Jerusalem and the cities of Judah, against which you have been angry these seventy years?' ¹³ And the LORD answered gracious and comforting words to the angel who talked with me. ¹⁴ So the angel who talked with me said to me, 'Cry out, Thus says the LORD of hosts: I am exceedingly jealous for Jerusalem and for Zion. ¹⁵ And I am exceedingly angry with the nations that are at ease; for while I was angry but a little, they furthered the disaster. ¹⁶ Therefore, thus says the LORD, I have returned to Jerusalem with mercy; my house shall be built in it, declares the LORD of hosts, and the measuring line shall be stretched out over Jerusalem. ¹⁷ Cry out again, Thus says the LORD of hosts: My cities shall again overflow with prosperity, and the LORD will again comfort Zion and again choose Jerusalem.'"

A Vision of Horns and Craftsmen

¹⁸ And I lifted my eyes and saw, and behold, four horns! ¹⁹ And I said to the angel who talked with me, "What are these?" And he said to me, "These are the horns that have scattered Judah, Israel, and Jerusalem." ²⁰ Then the LORD showed me four craftsmen. ²¹ And I said, "What are these coming to do?" He said, "These are the horns that scattered Judah, so that no

one raised his head. And these have come to terrify them, to cast down the horns of the nations who lifted up their horns against the land of Judah to scatter it."

A Vision of a Man with a Measuring Line

2 And I lifted my eyes and saw, and behold, a man with a measuring line in his hand! ²Then I said, "Where are you going?" And he said to me, "To measure Jerusalem, to see what is its width and what is its length." ³And behold, the angel who talked with me came forward, and another angel came forward to meet him ⁴ and said to him, "Run, say to that young man, 'Jerusalem shall be inhabited as villages without walls, because of the multitude of people and livestock in it. ⁵And I will be to her a wall of fire all around, declares the Lord, and I will be the glory in her midst.'"

⁶Up! Up! Flee from the land of the north, declares the Lord. For I have spread you abroad as the four winds of the heavens, declares the Lord. ⁷Up! Escape to Zion, you who dwell with the daughter of Babylon. ⁸For thus said the Lord of hosts, after his glory sent me to the nations who plundered you, for he who touches you touches the apple of his eye: ⁹"Behold, I will shake my hand over them, and they shall become plunder for those who served them. Then you will know that the Lord of hosts has sent me. ¹⁰Sing and rejoice, O daughter of Zion, for behold, I come and I will dwell in your midst, declares the Lord. ¹¹And many nations shall join themselves to the Lord in that day, and shall be my people. And I will dwell in your midst, and you shall know that the Lord of hosts has sent me to you. ¹²And the Lord will inherit Judah as his portion in the holy land, and will again choose Jerusalem."

> I WILL BE THE **Glory** IN HER MIDST
>
> ZECHARIAH 2:5

¹³ Be silent, all flesh, before the LORD, for he has roused himself from his holy dwelling.

A Vision of Joshua the High Priest

3 Then he showed me Joshua the high priest standing before the angel of the LORD, and Satan standing at his right hand to accuse him. ² And the LORD said to Satan, "The LORD rebuke you, O Satan! The LORD who has chosen Jerusalem rebuke you! Is not this a brand plucked from the fire?" ³ Now Joshua was standing before the angel, clothed with filthy garments. ⁴ And the angel said to those who were standing before him, "Remove the filthy garments from him." And to him he said, "Behold, I have taken your iniquity away from you, and I will clothe you with pure vestments." ⁵ And I said, "Let them put a clean turban on his head." So they put a clean turban on his head and clothed him with garments. And the angel of the LORD was standing by.

⁶ And the angel of the LORD solemnly assured Joshua, ⁷ "Thus says the LORD of hosts: If you will walk in my ways and keep my charge, then you shall rule my house and have charge of my courts, and I will give you the right of access among those who are standing here. ⁸ Hear now, O Joshua the high priest, you and your friends who sit before you, for they are men who are a sign: behold, I will bring my servant the Branch. ⁹ For behold, on the stone that I have set before Joshua, on a single stone with seven eyes, I will engrave its inscription, declares the LORD of hosts, and I will remove the iniquity of this land in a single day. ¹⁰ In that day, declares the LORD of hosts, every one of you will invite his neighbor to come under his vine and under his fig tree."

A Vision of a Golden Lampstand

4 And the angel who talked with me came again and woke me, like a man who is awakened out of his sleep. **²**And he said to me, "What do you see?" I said, "I see, and behold, a lampstand all of gold, with a bowl on the top of it, and seven lamps on it, with seven lips on each of the lamps that are on the top of it. **³**And there are two olive trees by it, one on the right of the bowl and the other on its left." **⁴**And I said to the angel who talked with me, "What are these, my lord?" **⁵**Then the angel who talked with me answered and said to me, "Do you not know what these are?" I said, "No, my lord." **⁶**Then he said to me, "This is the word of the Lord to Zerubbabel: Not by might, nor by power, but by my Spirit, says the Lord of hosts. **⁷**Who are you, O great mountain? Before Zerubbabel you shall become a plain. And he shall bring forward the top stone amid shouts of 'Grace, grace to it!'"

⁸ Then the word of the Lord came to me, saying, **⁹** "The hands of Zerubbabel have laid the foundation of this house; his hands shall also complete it. Then you will know that the Lord of hosts has sent me to you. **¹⁰** For whoever has despised the day of small things shall rejoice, and shall see the plumb line in the hand of Zerubbabel.

"These seven are the eyes of the Lord, which range through the whole earth." **¹¹** Then I said to him, "What are these two olive trees on the right and the left of the lampstand?" **¹²** And a second time I answered and said to him, "What are these two branches of the olive trees, which are beside the two golden pipes from which the golden oil is poured out?" **¹³** He said to me, "Do you not know what these are?" I said, "No, my lord." **¹⁴** Then he said, "These are the two anointed ones who stand by the Lord of the whole earth."

A Vision of a Flying Scroll

5 Again I lifted my eyes and saw, and behold, a flying scroll! ² And he said to me, "What do you see?" I answered, "I see a flying scroll. Its length is twenty cubits, and its width ten cubits." ³ Then he said to me, "This is the curse that goes out over the face of the whole land. For everyone who steals shall be cleaned out according to what is on one side, and everyone who swears falsely shall be cleaned out according to what is on the other side. ⁴ I will send it out, declares the LORD of hosts, and it shall enter the house of the thief, and the house of him who swears falsely by my name. And it shall remain in his house and consume it, both timber and stones."

A Vision of a Woman in a Basket

⁵ Then the angel who talked with me came forward and said to me, "Lift your eyes and see what this is that is going out." ⁶ And I said, "What is it?" He said, "This is the basket that is going out." And he said, "This is their iniquity in all the land." ⁷ And behold, the leaden cover was lifted, and there was a woman sitting in the basket! ⁸ And he said, "This is Wickedness." And he thrust her back into the basket, and thrust down the leaden weight on its opening.

⁹ Then I lifted my eyes and saw, and behold, two women coming forward! The wind was in their wings. They had wings like the wings of a stork, and they lifted up the basket between earth and heaven. ¹⁰ Then I said to the angel who talked with me, "Where are they taking the basket?" ¹¹ He said to me, "To the land of Shinar, to build a house for it. And when this is prepared, they will set the basket down there on its base."

A Vision of Four Chariots

6 Again I lifted my eyes and saw, and behold, four chariots came out from between two mountains. And the mountains were mountains of bronze. ² The first chariot had red horses, the second black horses, ³ the third white horses, and the fourth chariot dappled horses—all of them strong. ⁴ Then I answered and said to the angel who talked with me, "What are these, my lord?" ⁵ And the angel answered and said to me, "These are going out to the four winds of heaven, after presenting themselves before the Lord of all the earth. ⁶ The chariot with the black horses goes toward the north country, the white ones go after them, and the dappled ones go toward the south country." ⁷ When the strong horses came out, they were impatient to go and patrol the earth. And he said, "Go, patrol the earth." So they patrolled the earth. ⁸ Then he cried to me, "Behold, those who go toward the north country have set my Spirit at rest in the north country."

The Crown and the Temple

⁹ And the word of the LORD came to me: ¹⁰ "Take from the exiles Heldai, Tobijah, and Jedaiah, who have arrived from Babylon, and go the same day to the house of Josiah, the son of Zephaniah. ¹¹ Take from them silver and gold, and make a crown, and set it on the head of Joshua, the son of Jehozadak, the high priest. ¹² And say to him, 'Thus says the LORD of hosts, "Behold, the man whose name is the Branch: for he shall branch out from his place, and he shall build the temple of the LORD. ¹³ It is he who shall build the temple of the LORD and shall bear royal honor, and shall sit and rule on his throne. And there shall be a priest on his throne, and the counsel of peace shall be

between them both."' **¹⁴** And the crown shall be in the temple of the Lord as a reminder to Helem, Tobijah, Jedaiah, and Hen the son of Zephaniah.

¹⁵ "And those who are far off shall come and help to build the temple of the Lord. And you shall know that the Lord of hosts has sent me to you. And this shall come to pass, if you will diligently obey the voice of the Lord your God."

A Call for Justice and Mercy

7 In the fourth year of King Darius, the word of the Lord came to Zechariah on the fourth day of the ninth month, which is Chislev. **²** Now the people of Bethel had sent Sharezer and Regem-melech and their men to entreat the favor of the Lord, **³** saying to the priests of the house of the Lord of hosts and the prophets, "Should I weep and abstain in the fifth month, as I have done for so many years?"

⁴ Then the word of the Lord of hosts came to me: **⁵** "Say to all the people of the land and the priests, 'When you fasted and mourned in the fifth month and in the seventh, for these seventy years, was it for me that you fasted? **⁶** And when you eat and when you drink, do you not eat for yourselves and drink for yourselves? **⁷** Were not these the words that the Lord proclaimed by the former prophets, when Jerusalem was inhabited and prosperous, with her cities around her, and the South and the lowland were inhabited?'"

⁸ And the word of the Lord came to Zechariah, saying, **⁹** "Thus says the Lord of hosts, Render true judgments, show kindness and mercy to one another, **¹⁰** do not oppress the widow, the fatherless, the sojourner, or the poor, and let none of you devise evil against another in your heart." **¹¹** But they

refused to pay attention and turned a stubborn shoulder and stopped their ears that they might not hear. ¹² They made their hearts diamond-hard lest they should hear the law and the words that the Lord of hosts had sent by his Spirit through the former prophets. Therefore great anger came from the Lord of hosts. ¹³ "As I called, and they would not hear, so they called, and I would not hear," says the Lord of hosts, ¹⁴ "and I scattered them with a whirlwind among all the nations that they had not known. Thus the land they left was desolate, so that no one went to and fro, and the pleasant land was made desolate."

The Coming Peace and Prosperity of Zion

8 And the word of the Lord of hosts came, saying, ² "Thus says the Lord of hosts: I am jealous for Zion with great jealousy, and I am jealous for her with great wrath. ³ Thus says the Lord: I have returned to Zion and will dwell in the midst of Jerusalem, and Jerusalem shall be called the faithful city, and the mountain of the Lord of hosts, the holy mountain. ⁴ Thus says the Lord of hosts: Old men and old women shall again sit in the streets of Jerusalem, each with staff in hand because of great age. ⁵ And the streets of the city shall be full of boys and girls playing in its streets. ⁶ Thus says the Lord of hosts: If it is marvelous in the sight of the remnant of this people in those days, should it also be marvelous in my sight, declares the Lord of hosts? ⁷ Thus says the Lord of hosts: Behold, I will save my people from the east country and from the west country, ⁸ and I will bring them to dwell in the midst of Jerusalem. And they shall be my people, and I will be their God, in faithfulness and in righteousness."

⁹ Thus says the Lord of hosts: "Let your hands be strong, you who in these days have been hearing these words from the mouth of the prophets who were present on the day that the foundation of the house of the Lord of hosts was laid, that the temple might be built. ¹⁰ For before those days there was no wage for man or any wage for beast, neither was there any safety from the foe for him who went out or came in, for I set every man against his neighbor. ¹¹ But now I will not deal with the remnant of this people as in the former days, declares the Lord of hosts. ¹² For there shall be a sowing of peace. The vine shall give its fruit, and the ground shall give its produce, and the heavens shall give their dew. And I will cause the remnant of this people to possess all these things. ¹³ And as you have been a byword of cursing among the nations, O house of Judah and house of Israel, so will I save you, and you shall be a blessing. Fear not, but let your hands be strong."

¹⁴ For thus says the Lord of hosts: "As I purposed to bring disaster to you when your fathers provoked me to wrath, and I did not relent, says the Lord of hosts, ¹⁵ so again have I purposed in these days to bring good to Jerusalem and to the house of Judah; fear not. ¹⁶ These are the things that you shall do: Speak the truth to one another; render in your gates judgments that are true and make for peace; ¹⁷ do not devise evil in your hearts against one another, and love no false oath, for all these things I hate, declares the Lord."

¹⁸ And the word of the Lord of hosts came to me, saying, ¹⁹ "Thus says the Lord of hosts: The fast of the fourth month and the fast of the fifth and the fast of the seventh and the fast of the tenth shall be to the house of Judah seasons of joy and gladness and cheerful feasts. Therefore love truth and peace.

²⁰ "Thus says the Lord of hosts: Peoples shall yet come, even the inhabitants of many cities. ²¹ The inhabitants of one city shall go to another, saying, 'Let us go at once to entreat the favor of the Lord and to seek the Lord of hosts; I myself am going.' ²² Many peoples and strong nations shall come to seek the Lord of hosts in Jerusalem and to entreat the favor of the Lord. ²³ Thus says the Lord of hosts: In those days ten men from the nations of every tongue shall take hold of the robe of a Jew, saying, 'Let us go with you, for we have heard that God is with you.'"

Judgment on Israel's Enemies

9 The oracle of the word of the Lord is against the land of Hadrach

    and Damascus is its resting place.
  For the Lord has an eye on mankind
    and on all the tribes of Israel,
2   and on Hamath also, which borders on it,
    Tyre and Sidon, though they are very wise.
3   Tyre has built herself a rampart
    and heaped up silver like dust,
    and fine gold like the mud of the streets.
4   But behold, the Lord will strip her of her possessions
    and strike down her power on the sea,
    and she shall be devoured by fire.

5   Ashkelon shall see it, and be afraid;
    Gaza too, and shall writhe in anguish;
    Ekron also, because its hopes are confounded.

The king shall perish from Gaza;
    Ashkelon shall be uninhabited;
6 a mixed people shall dwell in Ashdod,
    and I will cut off the pride of Philistia.
7 I will take away its blood from its mouth,
    and its abominations from between its teeth;
it too shall be a remnant for our God;
    it shall be like a clan in Judah,
    and Ekron shall be like the Jebusites.
8 Then I will encamp at my house as a guard,
    so that none shall march to and fro;
no oppressor shall again march over them,
    for now I see with my own eyes.

The Coming King of Zion

9 Rejoice greatly, O daughter of Zion!
    Shout aloud, O daughter of Jerusalem!
Behold, your king is coming to you;
    righteous and having salvation is he,
humble and mounted on a donkey,
    on a colt, the foal of a donkey.
10 I will cut off the chariot from Ephraim
    and the war horse from Jerusalem;
and the battle bow shall be cut off,
    and he shall speak peace to the nations;
his rule shall be from sea to sea,
    and from the River to the ends of the earth.
11 As for you also, because of the blood of my covenant with you,
    I will set your prisoners free from the waterless pit.

BEHOLD, YOUR King IS COMING TO YOU; RIGHTEOUS AND HAVING SALVATION IS HE, HUMBLE & MOUNTED ON A DONKEY

ZECHARIAH 9:9

12 Return to your stronghold, O prisoners of hope;
    today I declare that I will restore to you double.
13 For I have bent Judah as my bow;
    I have made Ephraim its arrow.
  I will stir up your sons, O Zion,
    against your sons, O Greece,
    and wield you like a warrior's sword.

The Lord Will Save His People

14 Then the LORD will appear over them,
    and his arrow will go forth like lightning;
  the Lord GOD will sound the trumpet
    and will march forth in the whirlwinds of the south.
15 The LORD of hosts will protect them,
    and they shall devour, and tread down the sling stones,
  and they shall drink and roar as if drunk with wine,
    and be full like a bowl,
    drenched like the corners of the altar.

16 On that day the LORD their God will save them,
    as the flock of his people;
  for like the jewels of a crown
    they shall shine on his land.
17 For how great is his goodness, and how great his beauty!
    Grain shall make the young men flourish,
    and new wine the young women.

The Restoration for Judah and Israel

10 Ask rain from the L*ord*
in the season of the spring rain,
from the L*ord* who makes the storm clouds,
and he will give them showers of rain,
to everyone the vegetation in the field.
2 For the household gods utter nonsense,
and the diviners see lies;
they tell false dreams
and give empty consolation.
Therefore the people wander like sheep;
they are afflicted for lack of a shepherd.

3 "My anger is hot against the shepherds,
and I will punish the leaders;
for the L*ord* of hosts cares for his flock, the house of Judah,
and will make them like his majestic steed in battle.
4 From him shall come the cornerstone,
from him the tent peg,
from him the battle bow,
from him every ruler—all of them together.
5 They shall be like mighty men in battle,
trampling the foe in the mud of the streets;
they shall fight because the L*ord* is with them,
and they shall put to shame the riders on horses.

6 "I will strengthen the house of Judah,
and I will save the house of Joseph.

I will bring them back because I have compassion on them,
 and they shall be as though I had not rejected them,
 for I am the Lord their God and I will answer them.
7 Then Ephraim shall become like a mighty warrior,
 and their hearts shall be glad as with wine.
Their children shall see it and be glad;
 their hearts shall rejoice in the Lord.

8 "I will whistle for them and gather them in,
 for I have redeemed them,
 and they shall be as many as they were before.
9 Though I scattered them among the nations,
 yet in far countries they shall remember me,
 and with their children they shall live and return.
10 I will bring them home from the land of Egypt,
 and gather them from Assyria,
and I will bring them to the land of Gilead and to Lebanon,
 till there is no room for them.
11 He shall pass through the sea of troubles
 and strike down the waves of the sea,
 and all the depths of the Nile shall be dried up.
The pride of Assyria shall be laid low,
 and the scepter of Egypt shall depart.
12 I will make them strong in the Lord,
 and they shall walk in his name,"
         declares the Lord.

The Flock Doomed to Slaughter

11 Open your doors, O Lebanon,
 that the fire may devour your cedars!
² Wail, O cypress, for the cedar has fallen,
 for the glorious trees are ruined!
 Wail, oaks of Bashan,
 for the thick forest has been felled!
³ The sound of the wail of the shepherds,
 for their glory is ruined!
 The sound of the roar of the lions,
 for the thicket of the Jordan is ruined!

⁴ Thus said the LORD my God: "Become shepherd of the flock doomed to slaughter. ⁵ Those who buy them slaughter them and go unpunished, and those who sell them say, 'Blessed be the LORD, I have become rich,' and their own shepherds have no pity on them. ⁶ For I will no longer have pity on the inhabitants of this land, declares the LORD. Behold, I will cause each of them to fall into the hand of his neighbor, and each into the hand of his king, and they shall crush the land, and I will deliver none from their hand."

⁷ So I became the shepherd of the flock doomed to be slaughtered by the sheep traders. And I took two staffs, one I named Favor, the other I named Union. And I tended the sheep. ⁸ In one month I destroyed the three shepherds. But I became impatient with them, and they also detested me. ⁹ So I said, "I will not be your shepherd. What is to die, let it die. What is to be destroyed, let it be destroyed. And let those who are left devour the flesh of one another." ¹⁰ And I took my staff Favor, and I broke it, annulling the covenant that I had made with

all the peoples. ¹¹ So it was annulled on that day, and the sheep traders, who were watching me, knew that it was the word of the Lord. ¹² Then I said to them, "If it seems good to you, give me my wages; but if not, keep them." And they weighed out as my wages thirty pieces of silver. ¹³ Then the Lord said to me, "Throw it to the potter"—the lordly price at which I was priced by them. So I took the thirty pieces of silver and threw them into the house of the Lord, to the potter. ¹⁴ Then I broke my second staff Union, annulling the brotherhood between Judah and Israel.

¹⁵ Then the Lord said to me, "Take once more the equipment of a foolish shepherd. ¹⁶ For behold, I am raising up in the land a shepherd who does not care for those being destroyed, or seek the young or heal the maimed or nourish the healthy, but devours the flesh of the fat ones, tearing off even their hoofs.

¹⁷   "Woe to my worthless shepherd,
     who deserts the flock!
  May the sword strike his arm
     and his right eye!
  Let his arm be wholly withered,
     his right eye utterly blinded!"

The Lord Will Give Salvation

12 The oracle of the word of the Lord concerning Israel: Thus declares the Lord, who stretched out the heavens and founded the earth and formed the spirit of man within him: ² "Behold, I am about to make Jerusalem a cup of staggering to all the surrounding peoples. The siege of Jerusalem will also be against Judah. ³ On that day I will make Jerusalem a heavy stone

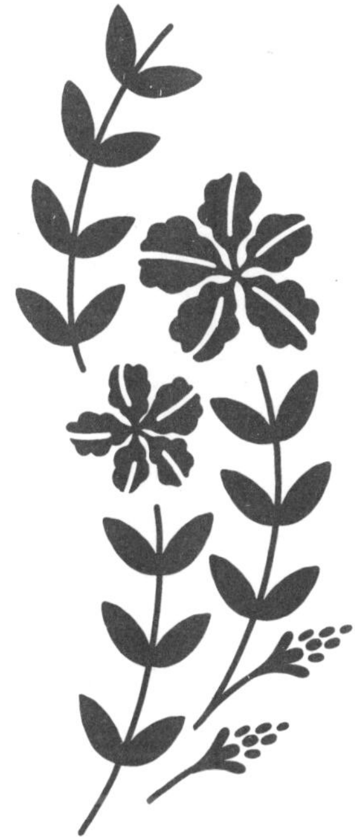

for all the peoples. All who lift it will surely hurt themselves. And all the nations of the earth will gather against it. ⁴ On that day, declares the Lord, I will strike every horse with panic, and its rider with madness. But for the sake of the house of Judah I will keep my eyes open, when I strike every horse of the peoples with blindness. ⁵ Then the clans of Judah shall say to themselves, 'The inhabitants of Jerusalem have strength through the Lord of hosts, their God.'

⁶ "On that day I will make the clans of Judah like a blazing pot in the midst of wood, like a flaming torch among sheaves. And they shall devour to the right and to the left all the surrounding peoples, while Jerusalem shall again be inhabited in its place, in Jerusalem.

⁷ "And the Lord will give salvation to the tents of Judah first, that the glory of the house of David and the glory of the inhabitants of Jerusalem may not surpass that of Judah. ⁸ On that day the Lord will protect the inhabitants of Jerusalem, so that the feeblest among them on that day shall be like David, and the house of David shall be like God, like the angel of the Lord, going before them. ⁹ And on that day I will seek to destroy all the nations that come against Jerusalem.

Him Whom They Have Pierced

¹⁰ "And I will pour out on the house of David and the inhabitants of Jerusalem a spirit of grace and pleas for mercy, so that, when they look on me, on him whom they have pierced, they shall mourn for him, as one mourns for an only child, and weep bitterly over him, as one weeps over a firstborn. ¹¹ On that day the mourning in Jerusalem will be as great as the mourning for Hadad-rimmon in the plain of Megiddo. ¹² The land shall mourn,

each family by itself: the family of the house of David by itself, and their wives by themselves; the family of the house of Nathan by itself, and their wives by themselves; ¹³ the family of the house of Levi by itself, and their wives by themselves; the family of the Shimeites by itself, and their wives by themselves; ¹⁴ and all the families that are left, each by itself, and their wives by themselves.

13
"On that day there shall be a fountain opened for the house of David and the inhabitants of Jerusalem, to cleanse them from sin and uncleanness.

Idolatry Cut Off

²"And on that day, declares the LORD of hosts, I will cut off the names of the idols from the land, so that they shall be remembered no more. And also I will remove from the land the prophets and the spirit of uncleanness. ³ And if anyone again prophesies, his father and mother who bore him will say to him, 'You shall not live, for you speak lies in the name of the LORD.' And his father and mother who bore him shall pierce him through when he prophesies.

⁴ "On that day every prophet will be ashamed of his vision when he prophesies. He will not put on a hairy cloak in order to deceive, ⁵ but he will say, 'I am no prophet, I am a worker of the soil, for a man sold me in my youth.' ⁶ And if one asks him, 'What are these wounds on your back?' he will say, 'The wounds I received in the house of my friends.'

The Shepherd Struck

⁷   "Awake, O sword, against my shepherd,
                against the man who stands next to me,"
                        declares the LORD of hosts.

TO CLEANSE THEM from SIN & Uncleanness

ZECHARIAH 13:1

"Strike the shepherd, and the sheep will be scattered;
     I will turn my hand against the little ones.
8 In the whole land, declares the Lord,
     two thirds shall be cut off and perish,
     and one third shall be left alive.
9 And I will put this third into the fire,
     and refine them as one refines silver,
     and test them as gold is tested.
They will call upon my name,
     and I will answer them.
I will say, 'They are my people';
     and they will say, 'The Lord is my God.'"

The Coming Day of the Lord

14

Behold, a day is coming for the Lord, when the spoil taken from you will be divided in your midst. ² For I will gather all the nations against Jerusalem to battle, and the city shall be taken and the houses plundered and the women raped. Half of the city shall go out into exile, but the rest of the people shall not be cut off from the city. ³ Then the Lord will go out and fight against those nations as when he fights on a day of battle. ⁴ On that day his feet shall stand on the Mount of Olives that lies before Jerusalem on the east, and the Mount of Olives shall be split in two from east to west by a very wide valley, so that one half of the Mount shall move northward, and the other half southward. ⁵ And you shall flee to the valley of my mountains, for the valley of the mountains shall reach to Azal. And you shall flee as you fled from the earthquake in the days of Uzziah king of Judah. Then the Lord my God will come, and all the holy ones with him.

⁶ On that day there shall be no light, cold, or frost. ⁷ And there shall be a unique day, which is known to the LORD, neither day nor night, but at evening time there shall be light.

⁸ On that day living waters shall flow out from Jerusalem, half of them to the eastern sea and half of them to the western sea. It shall continue in summer as in winter.

⁹ And the LORD will be king over all the earth. On that day the LORD will be one and his name one.

¹⁰ The whole land shall be turned into a plain from Geba to Rimmon south of Jerusalem. But Jerusalem shall remain aloft on its site from the Gate of Benjamin to the place of the former gate, to the Corner Gate, and from the Tower of Hananel to the king's winepresses. ¹¹ And it shall be inhabited, for there shall never again be a decree of utter destruction. Jerusalem shall dwell in security.

¹² And this shall be the plague with which the LORD will strike all the peoples that wage war against Jerusalem: their flesh will rot while they are still standing on their feet, their eyes will rot in their sockets, and their tongues will rot in their mouths.

¹³ And on that day a great panic from the LORD shall fall on them, so that each will seize the hand of another, and the hand of the one will be raised against the hand of the other. ¹⁴ Even Judah will fight at Jerusalem. And the wealth of all the surrounding nations shall be collected, gold, silver, and garments in great abundance. ¹⁵ And a plague like this plague shall fall on the horses, the mules, the camels, the donkeys, and whatever beasts may be in those camps.

¹⁶ Then everyone who survives of all the nations that have come against Jerusalem shall go up year after year to worship the King, the LORD of hosts, and to keep the Feast of Booths.

¹⁷ And if any of the families of the earth do not go up to Jerusalem to worship the King, the Lord of hosts, there will be no rain on them. ¹⁸ And if the family of Egypt does not go up and present themselves, then on them there shall be no rain; there shall be the plague with which the Lord afflicts the nations that do not go up to keep the Feast of Booths. ¹⁹ This shall be the punishment to Egypt and the punishment to all the nations that do not go up to keep the Feast of Booths.

²⁰ And on that day there shall be inscribed on the bells of the horses, "Holy to the Lord." And the pots in the house of the Lord shall be as the bowls before the altar. ²¹ And every pot in Jerusalem and Judah shall be holy to the Lord of hosts, so that all who sacrifice may come and take of them and boil the meat of the sacrifice in them. And there shall no longer be a trader in the house of the Lord of hosts on that day.

MALACHI

1

The oracle of the word of the Lord to Israel by Malachi.

The Lord's Love for Israel

² "I have loved you," says the Lord. But you say, "How have you loved us?" "Is not Esau Jacob's brother?" declares the Lord. "Yet I have loved Jacob ³ but Esau I have hated. I have laid waste his hill country and left his heritage to jackals of the desert." ⁴ If Edom says, "We are shattered but we will rebuild the ruins," the Lord of hosts says, "They may build, but I will tear down, and they will be called 'the wicked country,' and 'the people with whom the Lord is angry forever.'" ⁵ Your own eyes shall see this, and you shall say, "Great is the Lord beyond the border of Israel!"

The Priests' Polluted Offerings

⁶ "A son honors his father, and a servant his master. If then I am a father, where is my honor? And if I am a master, where is my fear? says the Lord of hosts to you, O priests, who despise my name. But you say, 'How have we despised your name?' ⁷ By offering polluted food upon my altar. But you say, 'How have we polluted you?' By saying that the Lord's table may be despised. ⁸ When you offer blind animals in sacrifice, is that not evil? And when you offer those that are lame or sick, is that

not evil? Present that to your governor; will he accept you or show you favor? says the Lord of hosts. ⁹ And now entreat the favor of God, that he may be gracious to us. With such a gift from your hand, will he show favor to any of you? says the Lord of hosts. ¹⁰ Oh that there were one among you who would shut the doors, that you might not kindle fire on my altar in vain! I have no pleasure in you, says the Lord of hosts, and I will not accept an offering from your hand. ¹¹ For from the rising of the sun to its setting my name will be great among the nations, and in every place incense will be offered to my name, and a pure offering. For my name will be great among the nations, says the Lord of hosts. ¹² But you profane it when you say that the Lord's table is polluted, and its fruit, that is, its food may be despised. ¹³ But you say, 'What a weariness this is,' and you snort at it, says the Lord of hosts. You bring what has been taken by violence or is lame or sick, and this you bring as your offering! Shall I accept that from your hand? says the Lord. ¹⁴ Cursed be the cheat who has a male in his flock, and vows it, and yet sacrifices to the Lord what is blemished. For I am a great King, says the Lord of hosts, and my name will be feared among the nations.

The Lord Rebukes the Priests

2 "And now, O priests, this command is for you. ² If you will not listen, if you will not take it to heart to give honor to my name, says the Lord of hosts, then I will send the curse upon you and I will curse your blessings. Indeed, I have already cursed them, because you do not lay it to heart. ³ Behold, I will rebuke your offspring, and spread dung on your faces, the dung of your offerings, and you shall be taken away with it. ⁴ So shall you know that I have sent this command to you, that

For **FROM THE** *Rising* **OF THE SUN** *To its* *Setting*

MY NAME WILL BE
GREAT
among the
NATIONS

MALACHI 1:11

my covenant with Levi may stand, says the LORD of hosts. ⁵ My covenant with him was one of life and peace, and I gave them to him. It was a covenant of fear, and he feared me. He stood in awe of my name. ⁶ True instruction was in his mouth, and no wrong was found on his lips. He walked with me in peace and uprightness, and he turned many from iniquity. ⁷ For the lips of a priest should guard knowledge, and people should seek instruction from his mouth, for he is the messenger of the LORD of hosts. ⁸ But you have turned aside from the way. You have caused many to stumble by your instruction. You have corrupted the covenant of Levi, says the LORD of hosts, ⁹ and so I make you despised and abased before all the people, inasmuch as you do not keep my ways but show partiality in your instruction."

Judah Profaned the Covenant
¹⁰ Have we not all one Father? Has not one God created us? Why then are we faithless to one another, profaning the covenant of our fathers? ¹¹ Judah has been faithless, and abomination has been committed in Israel and in Jerusalem. For Judah has profaned the sanctuary of the LORD, which he loves, and has married the daughter of a foreign god. ¹² May the LORD cut off from the tents of Jacob any descendant of the man who does this, who brings an offering to the LORD of hosts!

¹³ And this second thing you do. You cover the LORD's altar with tears, with weeping and groaning because he no longer regards the offering or accepts it with favor from your hand. ¹⁴ But you say, "Why does he not?" Because the LORD was witness between you and the wife of your youth, to whom you have been faithless, though she is your companion and your wife by

covenant. ¹⁵ Did he not make them one, with a portion of the Spirit in their union? And what was the one God seeking? Godly offspring. So guard yourselves in your spirit, and let none of you be faithless to the wife of your youth. ¹⁶ "For the man who does not love his wife but divorces her, says the LORD, the God of Israel, covers his garment with violence, says the LORD of hosts. So guard yourselves in your spirit, and do not be faithless."

The Messenger of the LORD

¹⁷ You have wearied the LORD with your words. But you say, "How have we wearied him?" By saying, "Everyone who does evil is good in the sight of the LORD, and he delights in them." Or by asking, "Where is the God of justice?"

3 "Behold, I send my messenger, and he will prepare the way before me. And the Lord whom you seek will suddenly come to his temple; and the messenger of the covenant in whom you delight, behold, he is coming, says the LORD of hosts. ² But who can endure the day of his coming, and who can stand when he appears? For he is like a refiner's fire and like fullers' soap. ³ He will sit as a refiner and purifier of silver, and he will purify the sons of Levi and refine them like gold and silver, and they will bring offerings in righteousness to the LORD. ⁴ Then the offering of Judah and Jerusalem will be pleasing to the LORD as in the days of old and as in former years.

⁵ "Then I will draw near to you for judgment. I will be a swift witness against the sorcerers, against the adulterers, against those who swear falsely, against those who oppress the hired worker in his wages, the widow and the fatherless, against those who thrust aside the sojourner, and do not fear me, says the LORD of hosts.

Robbing God

⁶ "For I the Lord do not change; therefore you, O children of Jacob, are not consumed. ⁷ From the days of your fathers you have turned aside from my statutes and have not kept them. Return to me, and I will return to you, says the Lord of hosts. But you say, 'How shall we return?' ⁸ Will man rob God? Yet you are robbing me. But you say, 'How have we robbed you?' In your tithes and contributions. ⁹ You are cursed with a curse, for you are robbing me, the whole nation of you. ¹⁰ Bring the full tithe into the storehouse, that there may be food in my house. And thereby put me to the test, says the Lord of hosts, if I will not open the windows of heaven for you and pour down for you a blessing until there is no more need. ¹¹ I will rebuke the devourer for you, so that it will not destroy the fruits of your soil, and your vine in the field shall not fail to bear, says the Lord of hosts. ¹² Then all nations will call you blessed, for you will be a land of delight, says the Lord of hosts.

¹³ "Your words have been hard against me, says the Lord. But you say, 'How have we spoken against you?' ¹⁴ You have said, 'It is vain to serve God. What is the profit of our keeping his charge or of walking as in mourning before the Lord of hosts? ¹⁵ And now we call the arrogant blessed. Evildoers not only prosper but they put God to the test and they escape.'"

The Book of Remembrance

¹⁶ Then those who feared the Lord spoke with one another. The Lord paid attention and heard them, and a book of remembrance was written before him of those who feared the Lord and esteemed his name. ¹⁷ "They shall be mine, says the Lord of hosts, in the day when I make up my treasured possession,

and I will spare them as a man spares his son who serves him. ⁱ⁸ Then once more you shall see the distinction between the righteous and the wicked, between one who serves God and one who does not serve him.

The Great Day of the Lord

4 "For behold, the day is coming, burning like an oven, when all the arrogant and all evildoers will be stubble. The day that is coming shall set them ablaze, says the Lord of hosts, so that it will leave them neither root nor branch. ² But for you who fear my name, the sun of righteousness shall rise with healing in its wings. You shall go out leaping like calves from the stall. ³ And you shall tread down the wicked, for they will be ashes under the soles of your feet, on the day when I act, says the Lord of hosts.

⁴ "Remember the law of my servant Moses, the statutes and rules that I commanded him at Horeb for all Israel.

⁵ "Behold, I will send you Elijah the prophet before the great and awesome day of the Lord comes. ⁶ And he will turn the hearts of fathers to their children and the hearts of children to their fathers, lest I come and strike the land with a decree of utter destruction."